D1255916

INNER CANYON

Where Deep Time Meets Sacred Space

INNER CANYON

Where Deep Time Meets Sacred Space

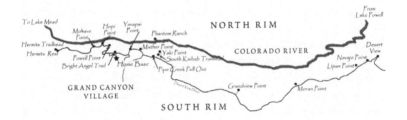

GAIL COLLINS-RANADIVE

LITTLE BOUND BOOKS

SMALL BOOKS — BIG IMPACT

© 2015, 2021, TEXT BY GAIL COLLINS-RANADIVE

Little Bound Books supports copyright. Copyright fuels creativity, encourages diverse voices, promotes free speech, and creates a vibrant culture. Thank you for buying an authorized edition of this book and for complying with copyright laws by not reproducing, scanning, or distributing any part of it in any form without permission. You are supporting writers and allowing Homebound Publications to continue to publish books for every reader.

Quantity sales. Special discounts are available on quantity purchases by corporations, associations, bookstores, and others. For details, contact the publisher or visit wholesalers such as Ingram or Baker & Taylor.

All Rights Reserved
Published in 2021 by Little Bound Books
Cover Design and Interior Design by Leslie M. Browning
Cover Images and drawn map © Milt Hetrick
Interior Map © National Park Service
Interior Icon: © Hannah Demel
ISBN: 9781953340122
Second Edition Trade Paperback

Little Bound Books is an Imprint of
HOMEBOUND PUBLICATIONS
WWW.HOMEBOUNDPUBLICATIONS.COM
HOMEBOUND PUBLICATIONS IS A REGISTERED TRADEMARK OF HOMEBOUND PUBLICATIONS

10 9 8 7 6 5 4 3 2 1

Little Bound Books, like all imprints of Homebound Publications, is committed to ecological stewardship. We greatly value the natural environment and invest in environmental conservation. For each book purchased in our online store we plant one tree.

DEDICATION

For Bill, who provided 'home base'
for this sabbatical work: thank you.

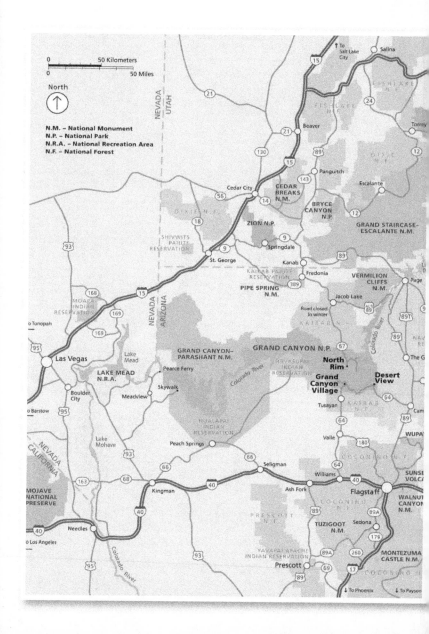

CONTENTS

FOREWORD
BY MELISSA GIOVANNI

*"When viewed in deep time,
things come alive that seemed inert."*
–Robert Macfarlane, Underland

*"If there is a point to being in the canyon, it is not to rush
but to linger, suspended in a blue-and-amber haze of
in-between-ness, for as long as one possibly can."*
–Kevin Fedarko, The Emerald Mile

For MANY YEARS, my relationship with the Canyon
was strictly scientific. I visited it frequently, first
as a geology student and then as a professor. But my
early visits consisted of driving to the edge and giving
a lecture on rock units, radiometric dates, depositional
environments, and its tectonic history before snapping a
quick picture and driving away.

Only after an existential career crisis did I start to experience the Canyon as a *place* (dare I say a sacred one) that was telling its own story. I then realized that I needed to stop talking and listen. This was about the time that I first met Gail at a political protest in Las Vegas. We hit it off immediately, owing to our mutual passions for environmental activism and for the Canyon itself. Although Gail and I encountered the Canyon at quite different points in our lives, our connection with the Canyon is remarkably similar.

I am not a religious person: I don't adhere to any organized tenets or believe in any gods. I find the scientific examination of our universe endlessly fascinating and fulfilling. And yet... I absolutely feel a sense of harmony when I'm out in nature, just as Gail does. I don't quite know what to do with the word "spiritual" —but I can't deny that the Canyon evokes a kind of universal understanding from a deep place within me. Some might call that a religious experience. Whatever you call it, this place is magical. It is ineffable. It is enormous and frightening and challenging and truly Grand.

If you are willing, you can be open to Gail's question: *"what might the Canyon have to teach that I need to know?"* She frames her journey through the lens of *geologic time*, a simple term for a difficult concept. It is easy enough to say that the Earth is 4.6 billion years old, that the oldest rocks in the Canyon are 1.8 billion years old and the youngest are 270 million years old, although the Canyon itself is just 6 million years old. It is vastly more difficult for the human mind to grapple with the implications of these numbers. The human timescale is infinitesimal compared to geologic time. Our species, *Homo sapiens*, has existed for just 0.005% of the Earth's entire history—and even that number is too small to really mean anything to us. Try this: imagine the Earth's history as a 24-hour day in which the Earth formed at midnight... humans will not show up until the final four seconds, at 11:59:56 pm!

In this context, how can we relate to a place like the Canyon? How do we traverse the impossibly vast gulf of deep time? We do it as Gail did—one step at a time. Pay attention to the rocks crunching beneath your feet, the raucous cries of the ravens wheeling above, and the whistling whisper of the wind in the pinyon pines. Slowly and carefully make your way below the rim, pausing to breathe and more importantly, to look. To listen. To smell. Above all, to *feel*. Feel gravity conspiring with the trail's unrelenting downward slope to pull you deeper. Feel your heart quickening as you try to make sense of the massive grandeur all around you. Feel your deeper self remember that you have always been a part of nature and that you *belong* here.

Geologically, the Canyon is both young and old. It is fresh and new to our eyes and at the same time inconceivably ancient. It exists wholly beyond humanity and has no need of us. And yet we need it. It seems fitting that Gail invited me to reflect on the Canyon's meaning in the midst of the Covid-19 pandemic. This has been (and still is) a time when I yearn for the peace of the Canyon more than ever. The century known as 2020 has been the trial of our souls in an era where each day seems to test our very will. Although I haven't seen the Canyon for many months, I draw strength from it by remembering the colors of the rocks, the sound of its silence, the whisper of the river, and the roar of the rapids.

When the way seems shut, another path reveals itself and there is always a way forward. I did not come to the Canyon intending to be changed. Indeed, most of my early visits left me awed but not humbled. But the Grand Canyon is both unchanging and ever-changing and it has changed me. It has humbled me. Whether you have been here before or are visiting for the first time via this book, accompany Gail on her journey and let the Canyon humble you.

The Grand Canyon is a master class in resilience in the face of constant erosion. It is an icon of permanence even though cracks appear everywhere and collapse seems imminent. It is our reminder that change is inevitable but adaptation is possible.

–*Melissa Giovanni, Ph.D.*
Guide and Instructor, Grand Canyon Conservancy
Las Vegas, NV | Autumn 2020

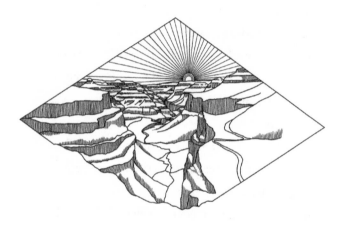

1

SPELLBOUND

"To speak of the universe's origin is to bring to mind the great silent fire at the beginning of time. We can see the dawn of the universe because the light from its edges reaches us only now, after traveling twenty billion years to get here."
—Brian Swimme

WHEN THE WHEATON VAN LINES driver phoned early on that Sunday morning to say that he couldn't find anyone to help offload my 5000 pounds of household goods (mostly books), I suddenly had a whole day ahead of me, with nothing I could be doing to settle into my newest apartment. Of course, I could have gone to the lay-led service being held at my new interim church in Flagstaff, AZ.

But there is church, and then there's Church.

Like my Unitarian Transcendentalist forebears, my inner life is grounded in the natural world, and so I packed up snacks and bottles of water and headed out of town, for a mere seventy miles away was the South Rim of the Grand Canyon.

I had been there before, several years earlier, and had even visited the North Rim a few years previously. After all, this is *the* place of pilgrimage that most Americans feel compelled to visit at least once in their lifetimes.

But I was totally unprepared for what would come to pass this time. This time, when I got out of the car and walked up to the Rim at Mather Point, the sight of the Canyon made me gasp. I felt I was being held by the throat and was choking.

Breathe, I told myself, just try to breathe. I walked along the paved path leading away from the main viewing area, seeking a place for solitary reflection. The August sun was hot so I sought out a spot shaded by a twisted juniper tree.

As I sat staring out across that great gash in our Earth, I sensed I was at an intersection of deep time and sacred space, and suddenly I began sobbing uncontrollably.

Was I 'losing it?' I looked around at my fellow tourists for clues: was anyone else experiencing what I was?

What about the middle-aged father talking nonstop and berating his young son for not seeing the castle of stone on the butte "right there next to the big titty!"

Or the grandmother having a meltdown when her family went out to the edge for a better look, until they turned their attention away from the view and put it back where it rightfully belonged: on her.

For truth be told, few people seemed to be really looking into the Canyon very much at all. Rather, after being surprised by the squirrels and amazed by the ravens, folks were dashing into the curio shops to buy some memento of their visit.

I would later learn that the average visitor's stay at the Canyon's rim is less than eleven minutes per person.

I too could/should just get back into my car and retreat to the safety of my still empty apartment in Flagstaff.

Instead, I spent the rest of the day driving along the east rim, stopping and staring, and sobbing at each pull off.

All across the great chasm, the changing afternoon light played like child gone wild with a box of crayons, turning the beige layer of Coconino Sandstone luminous, washing the Redwall into an innocent pink given depth and texture by shadows of brooding blue, then smearing a suggestion of green sage across the slope before dropping off into blackness as the inner canyon descended to the blue-green ribbon of river that could barely be glimpsed from the Rim at certain points.

Breathe. Just keep breathing! From Grandview Point to Moran Point to Lipan Point to Navajo Point, I became so increasingly intoxicated that by the time I reached the final pull off at Desert View, I was a drunken, blithering idiot!

When I could pull myself together long enough, I found a pay phone and called each of my daughters on my phone card.

"Yes, yes, I made it to Arizona. No, I'm not in Flagstaff. Actually, you won't believe this, but the Grand Canyon is practically in my new neighborhood...," I blathered into lines stretching westward to Washington, eastward to Tennessee.

My daughters were polite, if under impressed. Clearly one had to be here to appreciate this world-class wonder, to be having this first-hand experience that I simply couldn't get enough of!

So I circled back to where I'd started out so many hours earlier. Watching the sun drop down into and the full moon rise up out of the Canyon simultaneously, I intuitively knew that everything in my life was being turned upside down.

While watching the sun crest the Rim, it hit me in a whole new way what the science of our day has been telling us….that we are, in the words of mathematical cosmologist Brian Swimme, in his book, *The Universe is a Green Dragon*:

> "…*the first humans to look into the night sky and see the birth of stars, the birth of galaxies, the birth of the cosmos as a whole.*"
>
> And thus "*Our future as* a species will be forged within this new story of the world.*"

This was a new story, indeed...one to rival the one I grew up with that began with "Let there be light!"

> "To speak of the universe's origin is to bring to mind the great silent fire at the beginning of time. We can see the dawn of the universe because the light from its edges reaches us only now, after traveling twenty billion years to get here. We can now see the beginnings of time. We are the first generation to live with an empirical view of the origin of the universe."

I had long been trying to translate this new knowing into what it meant for how we people might live our lives. Did the Canyon hold clues, with its exposed record of the planet balanced between the sun and our moon, to a new world view? Was that why I felt I was under its spell?

Blessedly, darkness finally descended, erasing the Canyon, and releasing me to make my way home to my empty apartment, and my newest interim ministry position.

2

OMEGA TO ALPHA

"The galactic evolutionary process of the universe, the geobiological evolutionary processes of the Earth, and the cultural evolutionary processes of the human need to be understood, and celebrated, as three components of the single evolutionary narrative."

–Thomas Berry

FROM THEN ON, ON EACH MONDAY, (a minister's day off) I drove the seventy miles up to the Canyon to sit on the Rim and wonder....and weep...always the weeping.... but why? Was I about to get close to something truly significant?

Over the next months, I read everything I could get my hands on about the Canyon: its history, geology, geography, as well as narratives of exploration and adventure.

Whenever I was up at the Canyon, I attended any available Ranger program. In one such talk, the Ranger described the Canyon's five dimensions as being those of width, depth, length, time, and the ineffable: that sense of awe, grandeur, and beauty that takes ones breath away.

I felt both captivated and captured by this beauty, and by November found myself offering to stay on for a second year of interim work in Flagstaff, which was on a two-year schedule... if I could continue on a part time basis. This would give me more time up at the Canyon, time taken as a sabbatical after seven intense years of ministry.

I had no idea how/if things would work out, or where I would stay, or what that would look like, but I'd been on a spiritual path long enough to be sure of one thing: if I am meant to be doing something, it is better to 'go with the flow' rather than go 'kicking and screaming.' I was sick and tired of ending up bruised and bloodied!

So I floated the idea out into the universe and waited for the church board and the authorities back at headquarters in Boston to work out whether and how I was to stay on here.

By Christmas, I had a part-time contract negotiated for the second year. I'd willingly adjust my living expenses accordingly.

Winter had set in, bringing snow to northern Arizona. With the tourists staying home and the shuttle buses stopped, the west Rim loop was reopened to general traffic.

The pullout points along the Rim from the village out to Hermits Rest offered spectacular views of the Canyon. A favorite soon became Powell Point, named for the earliest white man to explore this area by running the Colorado River through the Canyon. His memorial rises appropriately enough like a pyramid situated on a bluff with a panoramic view.

Sitting up there shivering in the cold, watching the fog rise up from the River to meet the snow's falling down around me, I wept with the sheer wonder of it all…..and wondered whether I'd ever go below the Rim. What was I waiting for…a special invitation?

Well, yes: descending into the Canyon felt like treading on hallowed ground, and I needed to feel that the Canyon was inviting me into that particular intimacy.

Meanwhile, I'd simply drive the west loop, walk the Rim a bit at each pullout, and hang out beside the fireplace in Hermits Rest gift shop, a stone building that carefully blended into the canyon landscape, thanks to the mission and vision of the architect Mary Colter. There I began to hear the narratives.

The people who'd come over the years to work at the Canyon each had their own unique story, yet there was a common thread running through them. For instance, the man working the cash register at Hermits Rest was fairly typical: he came up here to hike one summer, and never went home. He found work that would support the minimal expenses of living here so that he could explore the area, and would stay as long as, well, what?

A couple who had been the first caretakers of the El Tovar Hotel in Grand Canyon Village even requested they be buried with a view of the South Rim and the village. Their headstone reads:

"IN THIS PLACE DOUBT IS IMPOSSIBLE.
ELSE, WHY ALL THESE WONDERS, THIS BEAUTY,
THIS GRANDEUR, THIS DEEP PEACE, THIS CONFIDENT
REPOSE? NO, HERE IS THE SPIRIT OF GOD,
HERE ONE MUST BELIEVE."
–CHARLES A. BRANDT, 1920.

Clearly the mystique of this place had smitten many. Another story was that of a photographer who called the church in Flagstaff and asked to speak with the minister. When the office manager put him through, he told me about his work and a life-threatening illness he had recently survived and wanted to know about attending our services.

Because I came up to the Canyon every Monday, I promised to bring him a packet of information, which I tried to do. But he was not around that particular Monday, nor was he answering his cell phone. So I found a gift shop that was selling his work and asked to leave the materials for him there.

Almost as soon as the clerk disappeared with the packet, another employee popped out of the office and informed me that he too was interested in attending the church in Flagstaff: he had heard about my arrival on public radio.

At one time a minister himself, this retired psycho-therapist had come up to work at the Canyon nearly seven years earlier because he needed to be 'in a place of awe.' He, too, worked for minimum wages and lived meagerly, so that he could hike into the Canyon on his days off.

Because his days off were mid-week, he hadn't been able to attend Sunday worship in Flagstaff. But the schedule was about to change, and he was requesting Sundays and Mondays off, hoping to reconnect with a congregation. Expecting to start coming to church at the beginning of February, he phoned the office to let me know his schedule hadn't yet been changed, and asked if I would bring him a copy of the sermon he had missed. I did that.

Over lunch he talked about his experiences in the Canyon, and when I shared that I was hoping to hike into it myself one day, he responded with: "Let's do it!"

And so, there I was: presented with an experienced hiking companion as if by the Canyon itself! It must finally be time to go below the Rim.

I chose my 60th birthday as the first day to make my way down into the Canyon.

After watching the sun set the evening before, then enduring a sleepless night as excited as a kid at Christmas, I got up before dawn to watch the sun rise from Powell Point, sensing I was about to begin a whole new chapter in my life.

For once I was glad to have a February birthday, for it's good hiking weather. Of course the snow-packed icy trail presented its own challenge, but my Canyon companion came prepared with a set of crampons and poles for me.

Starting down the South Kaibab Trail, I was surprised by the number of gray-haired people we were passing, in spite of its being a long holiday weekend when much younger folks would be off from school and work. There was clearly a fellowship of fit 'elders in residence' up here, many challenging themselves to hike from Rim to River to Rim while carrying camping gear on their backs.

As I navigated the steep descent towards the first switchback, my mind brimmed with words from Thoreau's essay on *Walking*:

"I have met with but one or two persons in the course of my life who understand the fine art of walking, that is, of taking walks, who had a genius, so to speak, for sauntering: which word is beautifully derived from idle people who roved about the country in the middle ages, and asked charity under the pretense of going *a la Sainte Terre*, to the Holy Land, 'til the children exclaimed, 'There goes a Sainte-Terre, a Saunterer, a Holy Lander.'"

Stopping at the first place where I could safely step aside, I paused to behold this holy landscape, inhale the silence found just below the Rim. But I tried to just breathe and keep going instead of sitting down and sobbing in the sense of how right it all felt.

For suddenly this seemed very much like the stage of life in Hinduism that's set aside for going off into the forest to do ones inner work, a time that usually coincides with the arrival of the first grandchild, or the first gray hair.

I qualified on both counts.

Hiking on down to OOH AH Point, and then further downward, to Cedar Ridge, a mere three miles into the Canyon, evoked the essence of beginning a long pilgrimage that would be carried out over the coming year, one that could officially welcome me into elderhood.

For apparently there's an evolutionary reason we're experiencing longer lifespans: recent research shows that we humans have triune brains, each layer of which represents a stage of evolutionary development ranging from modes of basic survival through to feeling levels within the social world and finally to the ability for learning and rational thought. But we now know there's also a vast untapped area of the brain that "holds the wisdom of the millennia, the dreams of tomorrow, and the capacity for communion with the cosmos," writes Rabbi Zalmon Schachter-Shalomi in his book called *From Age-ing to Sage-ing* that I'd been using with elders in my congregations for several years.

It's apparently becoming clear that the elders of any society (our 'youth culture' not withstanding) are called upon to activate that latent brain potential that isn't quite ready for full development until the afternoon and evening of life. Was this to be the point of my sabbatical work: a time for cultivating an aspect of knowing that was not possible in earlier life stages?

Perhaps. But right now the main focus was only on how to get back up and out of the Canyon before dark. Guided by my companion's careful instruction and example, I learned to go only short distances at a time, so as not to get out of breath. As we ascended through multiple layers of Earth, I felt I was passing over a threshold.

By March the snow had given way to mud that finally dried out enough that we could try a short hike down Hermits Trail at the western end of the Canyon. Dropping below the Rim barely half a mile revealed the shock of rocks that were millions of years old, boulders encrusted with fossils from the most recent shallow inland sea that covered much of what we know of as the American West.

The first fossil I actually saw, and only because my companion pointed it out to me, became as a Rosetta Stone, a key to a whole new knowing. I reached out to what looked like the remnants of a clamshell and became aware of calcium touching calcium through the membrane of my skin and the flesh of my fingertip.

I spent the next hour scrambling over fossil ridden slickrock, stopping often to sit still and place my fingertip into the remains of a 265 million year old ancestor, marveling at the arc of Time this connecting of our lives represented: it was as if Omega were beholding Alpha.

And suddenly remembering the scene on the ceiling of the Sistine Chapel in which Adam's finger connects with God, it hit me: this is everyone's creation story, the narrative of life evolved from a yesterday that's yet present in today and while still emerging into tomorrow, and all contained within this amazing Canyon.

So David Brower was right! Never mind that he meant to be facetious with the full-page ads he ran in an effort to save the Grand Canyon from being dammed and thus flooded:

"SHOULD WE ALSO FLOOD THE SISTINE CHAPEL
SO TOURISTS CAN GET NEARER THE CEILING?"

This was in response to proposals before Congress
to 'improve' the Canyon with two 'cash register' dams
that would back up artificial lakes into 148 miles of
canyon gorge....a benefit for people in powerboats, it
was argued, because then they could get a closer view
the canyon walls.

"Submerged underneath the tourists would be part of
the most revealing single page of earth's history," Brower
went on to argue in his role as Executive Director of the
Sierra Club.

His outrageous ads cost the Sierra Club its tax-ex-
empt status as a nonprofit organization. And they
motivated public action that saved the Grand Canyon
from being further dammed and flooded.

Now I looked down the cliff face below me: what
might the Canyon have to teach that I needed to know?
After all, I too had been raised within the comforting

cosmology of *The Bible*, the very story so exquisitely depicted on the ceiling of the Sistine Chapel. My western mind could make sense of an origin story that spanned human history, but what to do about an evolutionary arc that has so long preceded our species we are merely the latest blip?

I could fully understand the disconnect felt by Canyon visitors who followed a Park Ranger out to the fossilized rock on the Rim. Standing amid the remains of life forms from hundreds of millions of years ago, while believing that the earth was created only 6,000 years ago, one either argued with the messenger or ignored the information.

But I served a faith tradition that was rooted in scientific knowing as well as grounded in first hand spiritual experience, so I simply sat in reverence among the fossils and communed calcium to calcium, despairing that my post-menopausal bones were leaching this essential element. I even laughed at the thought of ingesting some of this natural supply as an act of communion: take, eat... this is my body...do this in remembrance...

Instead, I committed to another way of increasing my bone density: weight-bearing exercise. From now on hiking boots would replace church lady shoes, at least part of the time.

My sabbatical seemed to be shaping itself. Was it to be a quest to understand and integrate this deep time into what we believe and how we behave? Instead of trekking the Himalayas as some of my ministerial colleagues had done, I'd wander the Canyon, and descend this lying down mountain, 'paying attention' to whatever this place might expect of me...

As the church year wound down, I began to prepare for my part-time sabbatical year at the Canyon by creating a little nest for myself in my companion's efficiency apartment in Grand Canyon Village. Merely one large room with a mini kitchen at one end and a walk-in closet at the other, it was just enough: Thoreau had half this space in his cabin on Walden Pond.

Summer set in with the high desert heat increasing on the Rim; at the River below the temperature was usually some 20 degrees hotter, so hiking was out until things cooled down.

Even before the monsoons arrived with their afternoon thunderstorms that bring spectacular lightning shows, fire became a danger.

Two controlled burns were scheduled near Grand Canyon Village. Such burns are now done periodically in order to clear out the underbrush and keep forests healthy. Lightning used to be nature's way of keeping the ecosystem going, for fire completes the life cycle of many ecosystems, with the ashes replenishing the soil and sunlight once again reaching the ground and causing dormant seeds to sprout.

In fact, between the ponderosa pines along the trail to Shoshone Point, there once was enough open space for horse-drawn wagons to pass through. Now the ponderosa pine forest of Northern Arizona is the largest in the world…a monotonous area of single species that has crowded out others and created a dangerously flammable duff on the forest floor. Thus we set fires on purpose; controlled burns help restore the natural balance, and prevent even more catastrophic fires when/if lightning strikes. But fires seem to have a mind of their own.

A nearby controlled burn suddenly shifted direction and threatened the populated area: we were advised to prepare for a possible evacuation. Choking smoke underscored the urgency, but the fire was contained in time to call it off, and reopen the park to visitors. But we breathed a sigh of relief a tad too soon.

By the next morning the wind had fanned the embers into flames that jumped the road and headed for the Rim. The Navajo hotshots were called in to augment the fire fighters already on site. At least one-third of the Rim trail between Mather Point and Pipe Creek pullout was charred black by the time the fire was finally put out; this time for good, we hoped.

Yet this destruction is a gift: monitoring this burned area on both sides of a paved trail for a full year of changing seasons, I'd get to witness its regeneration. I was already wondering what it would look like by next summer.

When it was finally cool enough to get back into the Canyon, there was the matter of collecting the right gear. The needs of the hiking, camping, river running crowd constituted an entire supply industry. For as it's been said: there's no such thing as bad weather, only bad equipment. Perhaps this is the human method of adaptation!

It was good to be guided through the maze of multiple offerings for nearly everything you could possibly imagine needing and more, preferably by someone who had learned from trial and error first hand what works and what doesn't. That could not only save you money, but also from making mistakes that could be far more costly.

Take, for example, the poles.

It seemed simple enough, choosing something to help with balance. But types included with or without handles, with or without anti-shock capability, with or without rubber tips. Most came with a lifetime guarantee, which, when beginning at age 60, took on a different perspective: perhaps I should register them in my new granddaughter's name. But she'll have to wait until I no longer needed them and I looked forward to using them far into old age...not only for keeping my balance, but also for resting on the handles, and for reaching things up on shelves that grew higher as became shorter.

I won't go on about buying the right hiking boots; let me just say that mine were so bulky that at first I would start down a trail Frankenstein-clumsy, unable to stop, until I got used to them. And then there was the variety of packs: fanny, back, hydration, day, overnight, etc. a different kind for each need.

Then on to hats, socks, pants, vests, parkas: all with at least five different brands to choose from, with each featuring something different in its unique design.

But sooner or later it was time to lace on the boots, but then I needed instruction on how best to do that so that toenails won't turn black hitting the boot end while going downhill. However, this means lacing them so tight it becomes a toss-up between damaged toe-nails and aching shins: black toes or shin splints. Such a dilemma! I took my chances with the shin splints, as they'd hopefully be less immobilizing in the long run.

The preparation process grew to a fever pitch over bunched socks, unbalanced pack, how many layers to put on, take off, to take rain gear or sun glasses or both, knowing how quickly the weather changes, how many snacks of salt and protein (don't forget to add the M&M's to the trail mix!), and what, there were only two packages of peanut butter crackers? Make space for the Kleenex, chap stick, small notebook with pencil, and hand wipes.

But finally it was time to stop futzing, and go!

3

TALKING TO ROCKS

"The macrocosm of a cosmos still being born has its counterpart in the microcosm of a human being assimilating into
wholeness its ever changing and enlarging experiences. The
counterpart of the vast universal theme of emerging consciousness is the solitary process of individuation in each
human person."

–John Yungblut

DROPPING BELOW THE RIM on the Bright Angel
Trail caught my breath: I paused and was
absorbed into something beyond my own finite self.

The cold wind on the Rim blew right through my
protective layers, but by the mile and a half rest stop,
I was pealing off a sweat-soaked turtleneck and fleece

hooded jacket, and being grateful for my light weight breathable pullover and windbreaker.

At the top of the Redwall Limestone was a landing spot for helicopters a few hundred yards from an emergency phone and a rest shelter. Statistically, there were over 250 rescues each year from the Canyon, and the warning posters depicted the typical hiker in trouble as a fit young male.

Still learning my limits, I turned back after a brief rest here, while my hiking companion went down another mile. It was a deal we struck: we fairly sprinted down to the point where I'd start back up, while he kept on going until he needed to turn around in order to make it back up before dark. We shared a snack of trail mix before he took off without me. I craved time for reflection, and so was glad to finally sit alone with the tiny notebook I carried in my pocket.

I also liked setting my own pace going back up, yet felt safe in knowing that someone would be coming along behind me in case I faltered. This freed me up to enjoy my solitude, and the Canyon.

Not yet quite half way between the Rim and the River, I looked down from the top of the Redwall; I couldn't even see the river, only several more layers of rock formations.

There was a steady stream of hikers coming and going along the trail below, through Indian Gardens and out to Plateau Point, as well as on the trail above. Why did we do this?!

I suddenly remembered a trip to Kashmir in the Himalaya foothills where I saw women, children, and men walking 20 miles over a glacier to a holy place dedicated to the Hindu god Shiva; coming from all over India, most had never been near snow before, and were wrapped in shawls and wore socks inside their sandals for protection.

Why do people put themselves out this way? Why was a once in a lifetime pilgrimage to Mecca required of every Muslim? Why, here in this country, do Native peoples still undertake a vision quest? Perhaps it's because something happens when you make the effort to meet god, the sacred, the holy, the spirit, half way.

Was hiking the Grand Canyon a similar kind of pilgrimage? For it was different being within the Canyon than it was standing on the Rim. The ahas! were harder won, more visceral, and deeper than a fleeting wow!, before fleeing from the wind back into the comfort of the car or shuttle bus. There was no easy return to normalcy from down here: it was a long trek up and out and back to the familiar.

My hometown poet Robert Frost once wrote that this land was ours before we were the land's; perhaps experiencing our Grand Canyon was a way to finally, fully appreciate this continent we call home.

I started my long ascent, grateful for each step I'd take in the sheer beauty of it all. Step after step, I stopped only occasionally in wonder and to wonder: what might Thoreau's essay on *Walking* mean in this context, especially at the beginning when he claims that "every walk is a sort of crusade, preached by some Peter the Hermit in us, to go forth and reconquer the Holy Land from the hands of the Infidels."

Who are the crusaders, who the infidels within this context? Which were we, here now? This seemed to be a worthy meditation as I made my way along the trail winding up towards the Rim, especially in those moments when the trail was hard and steep and I despaired that my legs would give out. The shortened poles helped: I pulled myself up over the knee-numbing steps and then rested on a boulder, startling a back-packer who came up alongside without seeing me.

He'd been in the Canyon for four days and was slowly reentering civilization. We alternated passing one another for the next mile, smiling and joking as we got closer to the Rim.

Not too soon.... not yet, I whispered to myself as each switchback brought me closer to the end of my 'walk.' Something brightly blue caught my attention beside the trail ahead; I assumed it was some plastic litter and was surprised when it flew to another part of the trail. A bluebird, it seemed to be leading the way along the path, like in a fairy tale I barely remembered from childhood.

This suggested that my journey was somehow arche-typal, that there was something to be grasped here, something for and about those of us whose spiritual life is grounded in Nature and who would rather hike on a Sunday (like today) than go indoors to a church. It had to do with reconnecting body, mind, and spirit with the natural world. Still, it was a relief to make it back to the Rim and then on to my companion's comfortable apartment.

Fall progressed as I dashed back and forth between the Canyon's mystery and my ministry duties in Flagstaff. During one trip, I spotted a bald eagle flying over the road just below Tusayan and had to struggle to get out of the traffic barreling its way up to the Canyon: rude and reckless people missing the show as they rushed to the Rim.

This made the third eagle I'd seen: the first one near this very spot, the second one flying over the Rim several days later.

Joining the Hawk Watch International folks on the Rim near Yaki Point, I marveled that remnants of the dinosaurs still claimed this air space; soaring ravens and turkey vultures watched the tourists watching them!

Yet everything since the Permian Extinction had long been eroded away from these Canyon walls: from dinosaur bones to evidence of small mammals mor-phing into wooly mammoths, along with any clue to the coming of humans.

But now the California Condor, our Pleistocene cousin, banked on its nine-foot wingspan and flew closer to the cluster of humans listening to the Ranger talk about her. Rescued from the brink of an extinction that quite possibly began when our ancestors killed off the mega fauna upon which this species depended for sur-vival, the condor is a curious being. And this curiosity nearly did-in the species: shiny silver bullets from hunting humans became part of the Condors' diet, causing a mas-sive die-out from lead poisoning. A few rescued remnants were now breeding within the Grand Canyon National Park, watching the humans watching them.

*   *   *   *

I awoke from a sound sleep when the drumming of the rain changed into the silence of snow. Morning light confirmed it: several inches of white had blanketed the area, and continued to.

Snowed in! Secret desire of every true introvert: to be cut off from carrying out the daily routine; to be given the gift of time out of time, for 'hanging out inside,' in John Denver's phrase. *Inside* meant more than in the house sipping a mug of hot chocolate in front of the fire.

Inside also meant inside of oneself, with down time for reflection....our human form of Hibernation. In parts of the country where snow is rare, snow days are savored as an unexpected gift.

But I found I just couldn't stay inside! Snow had always been part of my psyche and so of course I'd get dressed and get out to clear off my car before everything froze in the predicted temperature drop. Yet were I going to go to all the trouble of bundling up against the cold, I might as well walk over to the Rim, to see another face of the Canyon.

The hush of the snow came closest to the silence of the Canyon that most humans would ever come to know. I stood in the whiteout that was above and below me, wearing a black jacket and snow pants, black hat and gloves: a black mark dropped into the pocket of

Time. Standing on the Rim, with fog rising up from the Canyon, rubbing all out like a giant eraser, smudging the edge of everything, I found myself wondering: what if human history had never happened?

After all, all human history had been expunged from the record above this rim, here, where Canyon time ended 270 million years ago.

But now the Canyon too was gone! Totally disappeared! Tourists stood at the railings and stared into the mist in disbelief. The shuttle buses to Hermits Rest weren't running, due to the 'inclement weather.' So I headed east along the Rim Trail and dropped down a few feet along the Bright Angel Trail just to be within the Canyon, mist and all. Mud and snow and mule droppings made for unsure footing, and with the fog erasing the edges of the trail, it was way too dangerous to go very far, although some hikers were trying. My heart hurt for the folks who had come to spend a day at the Grand Canyon, only to get weathered out...... especially those who'd been planning their pilgrimage perhaps for years.

I returned to the Rim Trail with its disappointed tourists pointing cameras at the nothingness beyond themselves.

But there was a patch of lighter sky moving towards the Rim, and soon it illuminated a piece of the Canyon so briefly that most of the tourists missed it. The fog closed in again, but now that I knew it could come and go, I set out along the paved trail that'd been cleared of snow.

Sadly, few tourists made the effort; they'd gone inside one of the hotels, restaurants, or gift shops to wait out the weather, hoping it would clear before they were scheduled to leave.

Suddenly the mists of time parted, and I rushed over to the edge of the Canyon to look down, surprised that I could see the whole of the second part of the trail I'd hiked at the start of the week....my own first hand trek into that vast entity outside of us and yet also within us in which we live and move and have our Being. And all at once I was clearer on why I must try to get ever farther into the Canyon, whatever it would take. There I might touch in with some of the oldest rocks on the planet and perhaps even experience the ultimate reality of the universe itself.

But meanwhile, confined to the Rim, I delighted in studying the sun's light playing off the Canyon walls: it changed every hour!

I moved with its moods by hiking the network of Rim trails, getting my legs ready for hiking into the Canyon when I could.

The light was enchanting! Sunrises and sunsets became special times ritually set aside to be present and pay attention. My companion joined me for sunsets, often carrying our picnic supper out to the special spots we'd found off the beaten track, away from the crush of people and their ceaseless noise. But sunrises were mine to enjoy in silence and solitude, after getting up and getting ready in the dark without waking him by tripping over him in his bedroll spread out in the middle of the floor.

However we choose to describe it, light becoming life is the powerful foundational narrative of our universe and solar system and planet. The uninterrupted evolution of light into matter into molecules into amino acids into cells into archea, bacteria, and eukaryotes into fungi, plants, animals including primates, some of which became our humanoid ancestors, increasingly capable of consciousness are all part of the golden thread that stretches smoothly and continuously from the initial Light of the Universe 13.7 billion years ago through Time to each and every living being here on Planet Earth today!

Light from our Star powered the dynamics of differentiation, subjectivity, and communion as species evolved in niches that optimized the Sun's energy. Here there were five different ecosystems in evidence within the one mile between Rim and River. Hiking down the seven miles of switchbacks was the biological equivalent of hiking from the Arctic to Mexico.

The most obvious ecosystem on the South Rim was the Ponderosa Pine forest, with its corresponding 'helpmate,' the Albert Squirrel. I spent hours watching this creature from the apartment window as it harvested the seeds from its tree: when climbing the trunk, it blended in perfectly with the swatch of tan on its back that matched the tree's (butterscotch scented) bark.

Its cousin on the North Rim, the Kaibab squirrel with its fluffy white tail, became differentiated in appearance over the 10,000 years they've been separated by the Canyon!

Mule deer moved throughout the Village freely by day, coyotes by night. The bugling of elks saluted Autumn's return with its golden warmth just in time for Halloween. We celebrated with a four-mile hike down the Hermits Trail.

Each STEP carried us some 20,000 years, unsettling my mind. Today's vegetation clung to yesterday's rocks; a little lizard skittered between the pre-dinosaur reptile tracks in the Coconino sandstone, warping Time.

Crossing the amphitheatre of Hermit's Shale, I took in the view of black varnish on the Redwall glowing orange in the sun, and marveled that the kinetic energy of the rocks builds up until it breaks down the face of the cliff.

Snowmelt and seeps erode the Canyon so slowly that a woman once complained to her son at the Rim: "It doesn't look any different than when I was here ten years ago!"

The two of us rested amid a grove of junipers. Were they twisted poetry, or petrified Mystics? All the current world religions include a symbolic Tree. I even had a glorious tree embroidered on one of my preaching stoles.

Joseph Campbell wrote that a tree growing in the region of present day Iraq is believed to be the Tree of the Knowledge of Good and Evil in the west, while in the east, it is perceived as the Tree of Eternal Life. Yet these are simply two 'branches' of the very same Tree!

Now a new image of the Tree is emerging.

"A tree is a self: it is more than it is leaves or bark, roots or cellulose or fruit. The tree, as a self, organizes all these millions of operations so that it can enter into relationships with air, rainfall, and sunlight" (Brian Swimme).

Now I studied a juniper decked out with smoke-blue 'berries.' Its realness filled up my senses, both figuratively and literally, as it exhaled the oxygen I needed to complete my energy cycle and I exhaled the carbon dioxide it needed for its life: clearly we inter-are, as the Buddhist monk Thich Nhat Hanh has so beautifully put it.

Or as Swimme himself suggests:

> "When you walk into a forest, learn to tremble with the magnitude of what you are about, and you will never walk out, for the you that approached the forest will be new; you will bear the presence of the forest with you. Sip a cup of coffee, and all the fir trees grow warm."

That thought sobered me, but right now I needed to focus on getting back out of the Canyon before autumn's early evening closed in on us.

Moving towards the winter solstice, I got up at each dawn's first light, giving in to an impulse to go out to watch the sunrise. Bundled up, I'd usually find the car so covered with frost that it took a big chunk of time to scrape it off.

Thus the sun was already well above the horizon and blinding as I drove out to the eastern part of the Rim. I pulled in and parked, positioned so that the rising sun was framed in my right side-view mirror, with the full moon setting on my left. The Canyon opened below as if it were a planetary intermediary between the sun and the moon.

The winter's atmospheric conditions closed the distance between the Rims, shrank the space between Rim and River, and created a sense that you could almost dip your toe into the Colorado. The Canyon seemed to be closing in on itself, and pulling me in along with it. I stumbled around on isolated Rim trails and whined into the depths: what if I were not smart enough, strong enough, focused enough, committed enough to bring forth whatever the Canyon was demanding of me?

But the Canyon simply persisted in being in my face: face it. Face what? I must be losing my mind! What was I doing, talking to rocks?

It was hard to identify with these anonymous rock formations: gendered gods and goddesses, namesakes of the buttes and bluffs out there, were so much easier to grasp.

Something in my own head, though not in my own voice, redirected my attention to a favorite movie...the Sound of Music, with its hills that are alive, a brook that trips and falls, the lark learning to pray....but these rocks were telling the story of planet earth for 1.6 billion years....

All I could do was pray/pay attention to the elements that formed us: the earth's evergreens and elk; the water's snow on branches and running over walls, the sun's fire in my eyes, while the air was creating thermals for the hawks to ride.

The lengthening nights pulled us back into dreamtime: at sunset, the deep blue and pink layers shimmered over the Rim where human history would be had it not eroded away. In its ineffable streak, I could almost imagine the possibility and promise that we wished one another at each winter solstice:

light, hope, peace, joy....we never sent out wishes for warfare, greed, chaos, misery....

*   *   *   *

During a long walk along the Rim the day after Christmas, we came upon groups of visitors standing still and looking at something: the marine fossil-studded rocks appeared to be alive, morphed into five bighorn sheep sunning on the cliffs.

As we humans peered over the Rim in amazement, pointing out the sheep to one another, we each came up with a different count. The male with its huge curled horns was easiest to spot: recognizable from the stuffed animals in the gift shops. The females were harder to see, blending in as they must on the blond colored bluff. Three were clearly there, but a fourth one was all but invisible in the foreground. They were not moving, making it hard to distinguish them from the rocks.

But there all alone out on the very edge of the ledge sat one small sheep...the 'black sheep?' or an introvert looking back over its shoulder and muttering "I don't know those creatures over there!" Why did the human mind need to project our inner stuff out into and onto the universe!! Surely the sheep was thinking no such thing! Its mammalian brain is limited to bonding with its band for survival.... Human brain layers are also programmed for survival: one visitor was using a gun sight to magnify the view. His wife claimed it was a Christmas present.

We were participating out of our bonding layer, those emotions that we were sharing as we stared, making us feel connected with one another, though in reality we were strangers.

Yet we humans also have the added capacity for creativity and imagination: pictographs and petroglyphs of bighorn sheep followed their species, and ours, throughout the southwest.

Now as we stood there staring, perhaps the universe was becoming aware of itself through us....sheep and humans alike!

4

BELIEVING AS SEEING

"The historic mission of our times is to reinvent the human at the species level, with critical reflection, within the community of life-systems, in a time-developmental context, by means of story and shared dream experiences."

–Thomas Berry

THE EARLIEST WHITE MEN TO MAKE IT TO THE RIM, the Spanish conquistadors back in 1540, did not 'see' the canyon because they could not integrate its reality into their world view: the counter-reformation Catholic theology of their day wouldn't allow them to.

Thus the Canyon would not appear on the old world maps of the new world for another 200 years!

When the Canyon finally became 'visible,' the American geologist Clarence Dutton named the buttes and bluffs, mesas and plateaus, after old world literature and religions because he thought the original Indian names were too ugly for such a grand landscape!:

Confucius Temple, Hindu Amphitheater, Temple of Ra, Shiva Temple, Temple of Osiris, Tower of Set, Trinity Creek, Isis Temple, Cheops Pyramid, Buddha Temple, Zoroaster Temple, Brahma Temple, Thor Temple, Ottoman Amphitheater, Wotan's Throne, Walhalla Overlook and Plateau, Freya Castle, Krishna Shrine, Vishnu Temple, Rama Shrine, Sheba Temple, Solomon Temple, Venus Temple, Jupiter Temple, Apollo Temple.

How ironically fitting, then, that today many of the major lookout points on the South Rim now bear Indian names:

Aztec Point, Havasupai Point, Apache Point, Hopi Point, Mohave Point, Pima Point, Yavapai Point, Yaki Point, Navajo Point, Shoshone Point.

The original peoples have inhabited this area since the last Ice Age, and it was theirs until the Powell Expedition in 1869. Harvesting corn and squash and beans (the three sisters) from the canyon floor, earliest peoples would also hunt bighorn sheep, deer and elk on the rim. Just below the Rim on the Bright Angel Trail there's a panel of pictographs, red spirals and hand prints that have graced this space since the Pleistocene. Native presence here today became more pronounced in autumn, even beyond the artifacts for sale in gift shops (rugs, pottery, baskets, and jewelry). Pickups lined the sides of the road, with family members scurrying around on the ground beneath the pinion trees, gathering up pine nuts.

In his scathing critique of the white man's religion, Sioux Indian and prominent scholar Vine Deloria described our American patriotism as an abstraction *about* the land, and reminded us that on this continent, *God Is Red.*

For its indigenous peoples, the land was sacred in all its aspects: every stone and bird and plant and animal was a concrete manifestation of the Holy, and was to be respected and protected accordingly.

Perceiving our country through the lens of peoples native to this landscape, rather than through the mindset brought here from the near-eastern religions by way of Europe, would mean shifting from the exploitative ('god' giving 'man' dominion over the world) to a more appreciative (the earth as an interconnected whole in which humans are but one part) point of view.

Inside the Grand Canyon Association's bookstore, a wizened Supai Ranger talked to us about the layers of canyon rocks, and how, if he touches each and talks to them while ascending the 7 miles from his home in Havasu Canyon, he doesn't suffer aches and pains when he arrives on the Rim. The black rocks are used in ceremonies and sweat lodges; the red rocks (which include the Redwall and the Supai group) are medicine to his people, as well as to all the indigenous peoples living in or near the Canyon.

He shared his gentle message about cherishing mother earth with the gathered children. Later, while walking along the paved path in the Village, I noticed a small boy, another member of the 'audience,' dragging his feet behind his father and beside his older brother:

"I don't think there should be shops and sidewalks along the Rim because that means they cut the trees down here," he lamented, "I don't think the Indians would like that."

His brother scoffed; his father wasn't listening...but he was lost in his own thoughts. I wanted to hug him, but didn't dare intrude.

Had the Canyon not received National Park status when it did, today it would be a platform for profit-hungry vendors clinging to the edge, clogged with privately owned and operated tramlines flung over the sides so that people could ride down the walls. Even today there remains a constant tension between those who, like Theodore Roosevelt, believe humans can't improve upon its grandeur so must leave it be for future generations to enjoy, and those who would turn the Rim into another Disney-grotesque enterprise.

Why we recognized the uniqueness of our landscape before it was too late is suggested by Stephen Pyne in *How the Canyon Became Grand*:

"(Our) national epic found its monuments, as often as not, in the American landscape. Nature, which America had in abundance, replaced the built environments that it lacked. Niagara Falls mocked the contrived fountains of Versailles, the Rockies dwarfed the Alps, the majestic Mississippi lorded it over a quaint Rhine, Yellowstone's geysers the lapdog hot springs of European spas. The natural, the big, the distinctive—all challenged the artifice of ancient and aristocratic societies."

Yet as more and more people have been drawn to this World Heritage Site, more stress has been placed on the ecosystems of the Canyon, especially from those who mindlessly littered, wandered off trail, and demanded more services.

I watched in dismay as a typical visitor, an overweight and obviously sedentary middle-aged woman, argued with the shuttle bus driver, demanding to be taken to the bottom of the Grand Canyon. "Sorry, Ma'am," he told her, "These buses don't go into the Canyon." "You mean I came all this way and I have to stay at the top!? How do I get to the bottom?" "Well, there are three ways: by foot, by mule, and by boat."

She recoiled in horror at the prospects of walking; riding a mule wasn't possible as she wouldn't make the weight limit; and river trips were booked years in advance, thus she was indeed stuck on the Rim....and quite indignant about it.

Meanwhile I sought out silence so I might listen to the Canyon rather than other people, but, as Robert Wallace described:

"Not a solitary sound emerged from the depths. It is as though all the hushes of time have drifted into the canyon and filled it to the brim."

I searched for silence out on Hermits Trail, and discovered instead the helicopter path over the North Rim....with the continual drone overhead. I hiked out to overlooks and always, everywhere, there was the sound of human voices.

Craving the Canyon's quiet, I dropped below the Rim on the Bright Angel Trail, only to discover that the noise in my ears was not just from the many people along this popular trail: it was my own voice responding to the wind and the ravens!

At mile-and-a half rest stop, while my companion continued downward towards the three-mile stop, I chose to start back up, gradually getting my Canyon legs into condition. But first, I wanted to sit still and just stare at the assortment of people, yes, but also beyond.

So I found an area to sit in solitude, and look off down into the Canyon, but could see little of the continuing trail from this tucked-away place. So I turned around and looked up.

The Coconino Sandstone rose as a solid wall in front of my face; I was amazed to be so close to it, after so many months of seeing it from the Rim, from where it looks like a bathtub ring around the Canyon. This formation is 275 million years old!! And I had already walked beyond it, another 50 million years, give or take.

Now I ascended up the Supai Group (315-285 million years old), the Hermit Formation's 280 million years, through the Coconino Sandstone for 5 million years, then on up the Toroweap Formation for another 3 million years, until I reached the top layer from which our human history has long since been eroded.

Slowly, taking my 'time,' taking it in, yet mindful of my companion's admonition to not sit and rest if I wanted to be able to do longer hikes into the Canyon some day, I just paused at overlooks, drank water, and looked up.

I allowed myself one sitting down time, when a string of mules passed by and I needed to get off the trail anyway. I perched on the edges of space and wondered about stepping off: would thermals carry me back up the cliff face like the condors, hawks, ravens, and eagles?

*   *   *   *

Winter wore on. Looking out the window into the cold drizzle of my childhood in New England, I recalled how I always had to go outdoors no matter how miserable the weather. We walked to school back then, and in spite of arriving cold or hot or wet, the time en route was always an invitation to collect one's thoughts, make a mental note of the little changes that signified a new season, and maybe even daydream a bit....

So of course there could be no question of canceling a bad-weather hike. Protective clothing has come a long way since the bulky snow pants we wore under our mandatory dresses and the heavy wool coats that got even heavier when wet.

We 'layered up,' beginning with a moisture wicking shirt, then adding a fleece jacket for warmth, and finishing up with a waterproof, hooded parka. Snacks and Kleenex stuffed in various pockets, liters of water loaded into a backpack, we started down the South Kaibab Trail into the fog and mist at a brisk pace that warmed us up quickly.

Despite the weather, the trail was 'crawling' with people doing what we people do: continually making noise. Was this noise our anchor to the superficial, an acceptable way to avoid the inner depths of ourselves, as well as that of the Canyon?

One man was videotaping his trip, and stopped to ask about rattlesnakes: I assured him that we weren't on their food chain, so he shouldn't worry too much about coming across any, just so long as he doesn't 'rattle' *them*.

I probably should have mentioned that they are still hibernating, for now. My cynicism was showing, and growing. I clearly needed an 'attitude adjustment,' a change in the mindset that has grown more self-protective and shadow-projective during my seven years of ministry, thus making this sabbatical so welcome, and essential.

Seminary had been for cleaning out personal baggage so as not to dump it onto congregants, but parish work activated ever-newer layers of psychic 'stuff' to come to terms with.

Walking has always been one way I've done some of this inner work, which is why I helped create a labyrinth on the grounds of a district run retreat center: walking has long been a spiritual discipline, a physical pathway to seek out answers.

But hiking here in the Grand Canyon was another kind of a 'walk' altogether!

Sauntering four miles down the trail took us an hour and a half, with a leisurely lunch break enjoyed behind a juniper so as to be sheltered from the wind. But then

there was the matter of getting back up before win-
ter-early darkness.

So we shortened our hiking poles and removed the
anti-shock adjustment so that we could use them to pull
ourselves up the steep parts of the trail...pealed off and
stowed a layer of clothes...popped two aspirins to prevent blood clots....and started up.

Going back up was nothing short of torturous. Just
making it one step at a time occupied one's thinking, and
by the time we passed the trail maintenance crew, the
only 'creative' insight I could latch onto was that perhaps
my taxes were going to pay for this work. For trails in
the National Parks are definitely part of the solution to
our sedentary lifestyle, such as this physical ordeal of a
slow, slogging hour after hour after hour...rounding a
bend into the cold, putting layers back on, having hat
snatched off by the wind, stopping frequently so as
not to get out of breath...until finally my companion
announced "only one more mile to go!" as if that were
somehow comforting.

It wasn't, especially when I looked up at the trail
that was a 90-degree angle exactly perpendicular from

where we were currently standing, and along which I could barely make out brightly colored ant-sized people wending their way slowly up the switchbacks rising above my head. The only real comforting thought I had was that by pulling my weight up the steepness with my arms on my poles I was building upper-body strength without spending time indoors at a gym.

But then, every once in a while, there came a brief glimpse of rainbows penetrating and punctuating the profound silence of the Canyon.

*　　*　　*　　*

Preparing for yet another hike took so much time and effort to get ready! The amount of equipment needed was daunting, from deciding which pack, how much water, what snacks, how many layers of clothing...until we were finally tromping towards the trailhead. I was mainly aware of how uncomfortable the boots were with bunched up socks and liners as I adjusted poles, affixed ice cleats to the bottom of boots, all while being watched by curious visitors:

"You must be serious hikers,' someone said.

I grimaced, feeling like a fraud for the short distance I'd be going, perhaps as far as the second set of pictographs, a mere two miles down....and two miles back up. But rounding the first switchback below the Rim I forgot the discomfort and let the Canyon take over my awareness.

Passing through the second rock tunnel, I found myself face to face with the Coconino Sandstone. Winter's atmospheric pressure made it seem so close it was blurry and I was dizzy.

Disoriented, I dissolved into deep time, became embedded within the rock's pages of evolution. Then a thought appeared out of nowhere: what if it's not about us?!

What if we humans were *not* the point of it all, the pinnacle of creation, the end point of evolution?

What if it were not about the young woman bounding up the trail from the River, five months pregnant, husband and sister in tow?

What if it were not about the elderly man from Florida, going slowly with a broken pole, for "there's no way to train for this where I come from, flat and humid and sea level air pressure."

What if it were not about the father and two young sons who have turned back because the littlest brother got scared and is waiting up on the Rim with their mother?

What if it were not about the group of Amish young people, wearing snow pants under cotton dresses?

What if it were not about the seventy-five-year old hiker out to beat his own records so he could write a book...did he ever even notice the Canyon as he hiked from Rim to River to Rim in so few hours?

For in reality, the top rock layer of the Canyon on the South Rim is 265 million years old: eroded away are the layers that include the time of the dinosaurs, the age of the wooly mammoths, and the eye blink of our human moment.

It was only at sunset, when the light streaked into pink layers above the Rim, that I could catch a glimpse of those missing eons!

After nearly a year of watching sunsets here, I'd learned to wait around long enough to watch what happens next. It could be a long wait, with not much promise of what might come, just a few stray rays of gold beneath the cloud bank. But that would be enough.

I climbed into the warmth of my car, out of the wind coming up from the Canyon, and continued to wait, and wait, until a hint of pink streaked through the gray, then wait longer, longer, still longer until finally, suddenly, the whole sky was a splash of splendor: pink red orange yellow combined into a color that would have challenged even the small boy in the Indian Paint Brush legend.

Color radiated from where the sun had been and out to the whole of the sky, taking our breath away, those handful of us humans who were still on hand to witness its vividness. It was as if the Canyon had become a ghostly extension of itself, with future layers of Time reaching skyward.

I was reminded of the Hopi concept of *tunayta*...a dynamic state of infinite becoming that de Chardin had called *cosmogenesis*.

A Jesuit priest-theologian and a distinguished geologist-paleontologist, Teilhard saw the cosmos as a holistic entity in process.

Was that also the promise of the Canyon? Were the past layers of earth's becoming that those of us watching sunset were present to but a prologue to future dynamics of the planet that we could barely imagine? Yet there were clues.

Hopi jewelry often depicted spirals. This seemed to reflect both the cyclical time of earth's seasons and the linear time of its history. But instead of a circle or a line, the true trajectory of the universe embraced both, spiraling forward and backward simultaneously, on microcosmic and macrocosmic levels conjoined!

As the last of the light dimmed the Canyon's profile, I lingered a while longer. The Hopi origin story took place somewhere within this space, a secret sight of emergence faithfully protected by legend. That narrative seemed right for this place, what with the emergent dimension of evolution manifesting in human creativity!

*   *   *   *

Like all spiritual paths, this one was not constant. I kept 'losing it,' regressing to a limited and limiting viewpoint. The dashing back and forth between Canyon and Flagstaff broke my concentration and any sense of continuity…so that sometimes upon my return, the Canyon was just a beautiful backdrop that didn't grip my imagination or disclose itself to me and I fretted that my time here would too soon be up.

And meanwhile, winter went on and on. Our spirits grew weary awaiting the latest forecast of snow: we were holding our breaths in expectation and anticipation and preparation. The storm kept organizing itself, then petering out, then regrouping with the moisture coming in off an ocean hundreds of miles away. Was it self-organizing on a macroscopic level, just as the coming snowflakes will do on a nearly microscopic/microcosmic level?

Finally it arrived: forty inches of new snow, and then it kept going, reminding me why fellow New Englanders threatened to move to Arizona. But this **was** Arizona, though not with the non-winter weather associated with the state.

It was truly beautiful, as the flakes floated down and the plowed piles rose higher than the tops of the cars, bringing a flashback to the February I turned 16 and learned to how to drive. I took comfort in knowing that if I couldn't stop the car, I could just steer it into the snowbanks lining the roads. The instructor was not amused.

Yet extreme weather seemed to be the only thing these days that had the power to disrupt our lives and call our attention to something beyond human control.

Up at the Canyon, the snow soon caused landslides that closed the Bright Angel Trail from mile and a half to Indian Gardens....an inconvenience only to a handful of hikers and mule riders, I supposed. But this was the erosion process, the major sculpting factor that created this infamous abyss. Snow and rain eroded the walls and caused rockslides the mules couldn't climb over; trips were cancelled for a month.

Upon finding the Bright Angel Trail was still closed, we headed for the South Kaibab trailhead, and started down in wintry conditions, glad for having crampons to navigate the ice pack. Within half a mile the ice was gone. By another quarter mile we were peeling off a layer of clothes: the sun was summery on my face and at the back of my neck.

An elderly man bounding up the trail called back over his shoulder to us, "You kids have a great hike." Being over 60, we haven't been called kids for a very long time!

Giving myself over to the hike itself, I got into a rhythm that felt like swimming on land...coming up from what once was a warm inland sea, salty sweat on my tongue, then feeling like a turtle or tortoise climbing over all obstacles with a steady unswerving pace.

By breaking my previous records for time in and out, I was in training, yes, but felt more like I was tapping into the Canyon's rhythm, reluctantly arriving at the final half mile, not wanting to be out of this womblike embrace.

*   *   *   *

With a slew of errands back in Flagstaff to get to, the tail end of the morning's news caught me off guard: the Bright Angel Trail had been re-opened to hikers. I'd give myself over to a mile hike, down to the start of the Coconino Sandstone, a sacred place for me.

I expected the trail to be crawling with eager hikers, but few folks seemed to know the trail was open. An isolated tourist ventured down the ice and slick rock, in sneakers, carrying a plastic back of treasures purchased from a Rim shop.

This was the quietest I'd yet experienced on this trail, the silence broken only by the sound of water seeping through the cracks in the rock walls, causing further erosion: the Canyon is still in the process of becoming by continuing to widen and deepen. I rested in its presence and wept.

5

BRIGHT ANGELS
AT THE RIVER

"When we experience consciousness of the unity in which we are embedded, the sacred whole that is in and around us, we exist in a state of *grace*. At such moments our consciousness perceives not only our individual self, but also our larger self, the self of the cosmos."

–Charlene Spretnak

F INALLY, IT CAME TO PASS: I wandered over to the Bright Angel transportation desk to check about getting on the waiting list for a mule trip in mid-February, and the Navajo clerk signed me up for the very next morning.

I requested a second overnight and got that as well. He weighed me in, as all riders must be under 200 pounds fully dressed. I qualified, and was handed my 'equipment.'

The bright yellow rain slicker with MULE RIDER in big black block letters on the back was the 'ticket' that would get me on the 'mule train' at 8 the next morning. Then I received two heavy-duty plastic sacks to make overnight items fit into saddle bags, plus a canteen with a packet of lemon juice to soak overnight so that carried water wouldn't taste of its lining.

I walked away, loaded up with my 'stuff,' incredulous and elated. I couldn't believe it may finally happen, that I might actually get deep into the Canyon....and more: that I'd get to spend my 61st birthday at the bottom. I had given up any hope of ever hiking all the way down and back up.

A three-mile Rim hike calmed me down enough to pack and then get some rest. Morning would come very early.

It was cold, overcast, threatening rain and snow as I gathered up my gear and walked over to the stone mule corral for orientation. My hiking companion stood with me until he needed to go on to work at Lookout Studio.

Orientation was both amusing and intimidating, with the emphasis on making us realize this was not a Disneyland adventure that was predictable and controllable: these were real animals with minds of their own… we were to treat them like substitute teachers reigning in fourth graders who'd been at recess for a month, the month the trail had been closed that these mules spent eating and doing whatever else mules do when they're not 'working.'

There were three strings of mules for three groups of riders. The first two groups were taken into the corral and matched with mules.....they were going down as far as Indian Garden and Plateau Point. We Phantom Ranch overnighters were sent off to do other things for a while, which mostly meant making a last-minute trip to the nearby pit toilet.

The sky was clearing within the Canyon as the first two groups started down; it could be a decent day after all.

Our group consisted of four women and one man: two couples and a single, me. We quickly learned that the male, a retired educator from the Midwest, had lost 60 pounds over the last two years in order to do this mule trip! He brought up the rear of our line: his wife in front of him, the other two women came next, putting me right behind the wrangler.

Her name was Sherry, and she was a tiny, wiry young woman with a long braided blonde ponytail. We immediately trusted her implicitly; there was no choice! I tried not to fixate on the fact that my mule was named 'Short Cut,' a tendency she has 'mostly gotten over,' Sherry assured me.

We started down the muddy trail, getting the feel for being up high on the back of a very large animal. Sherry stopped us at the top of the first switchback to check saddles and get our names down on a piece of paper.

By then all the orientation instruction had come to life and we had questions about holding the reins and how to use the 'motivators,' the whips that would urge the mules to keep moving in a tight grouping rather than lagging behind and then trying to catch up, which was so dangerous on a narrow trail with a sheer drop-off.

We continued along the three miles of trail I'd been hiking; I was impatient to get to the levels I hadn't yet been close to: the Redwall, for instance....down Jacob's Ladder, as the set of switchbacks through the Bright Angel Fault was called, to the wash that runs out to Indian Garden, our first prolonged stop.

With time out for a box-lunch break, we got off our mules with Sherry standing beside each of us in turn, to steady us. The first bit of relief was finding that my legs still worked...maybe I'd make it, after all.

When we were mounted up again, Sherry told us we were not quite even half-way yet, and we began to worry again that we won't be able to endure the plod through even the wash ahead. But at this elevation there were the spring wildflowers to distract our attention, after too much winter up on the Rim.

When stopped at a waterfall, I looked over my shoulder and asked about the trail dropping off a bluff...

"That's ours," Sherry confided. Oh. The others didn't see it until we began the grueling descent down the Devil's Corkscrew, a steep path through the Vishnu Schist.

Now the legs really felt it: it was as though I were trying to brake the mule like a car by bracing myself, with my legs taking the brunt of the downward part of the trip. By the time we finished crisscrossing Pipe Creek, where the water seemed to surprise the mules because otherwise it was dry so much of the time, the outside portion of my right knee had become excruciatingly painful, distracting me from the scenery. Bummer! But the first sight of the Colorado River revived the awe, reminding us all of the point of the trip.

Sherry warned us not to get our hopes up at first sight of the suspension bridge over the river; it was not the one the mules used to cross. The black bridge with its covered flooring that mules will walk over was another two miles away.

The River trail to it went up and down as it wound along the rock formations of the Inner Canyon. Flowing below and beside us, the Colorado was in its original state: the red mud from the winter snowmelt gave the River its name.

I tried to focus on being grateful to have this rare treat, but mostly I was looking forward to getting through the tunnel (duck), across the black bridge, and on around the bend to Bright Angel Creek and finally to Phantom Ranch.

We made it! As Sherry helped each of us dismount, we staggered over to the rest area and 'bonded' in our gratitude that we wouldn't have to get back on our mules for another two days...we were all two-nighters.

The ranch manager welcomed us. "The good news is you made it! The bad news is the water pipeline is broken so we're closing Phantom Ranch tomorrow at 8 A.M. You'll have to go back up to the Rim tomorrow."

Our groans of disappointment nearly drowned out the advice to go out and hike so that our legs wouldn't freeze up.

It was two in the afternoon; dinner would be at five: this left just three hours to see and do all that was planned for the full extra day down here. Where to start?

I headed for a trail that everyone says is a 'must' for its views of the Ranch and River. Following the Bright Angel Creek northward, I cut off and started climbing up towards Clear Creek overlook. But while climbing higher and enjoying the high desert landscape, it suddenly hit me: all this time I'd been striving to get to the River. So why was I hiking up and away from it, for yet another distant view?!

Turning around and retracing my steps, I followed the creek back through Phantom Ranch, passing the hiker dorms, the canteen, the cabins, the shower house. There were a couple tents in the campground. It was impressive that these handful of campers carried their equipment on their backs the whole way, some 18-plus miles roundtrip.

I walked up to and crossed over the suspension bridge that carries the water pipe across the river and up the opposite wall of rock, and celebrated the creative force of the Universe itself as it is manifested in human ingenuity!

A park helicopter buzzed down through the corridor between the Canyon walls, landed on a designated piece of beach, and carried off the pipeline workers. When the sound stopped echoing, the silence settled and I caught my breath.

Other mule riders appeared, all walking, walking, walking off their soreness. We briefly commiserated over our trip experience and the limited time here at the River.

Craving solitude, I headed back along the creek, found an alcove of rock to crawl into. Breathe, just keep breathing, I reminded myself....quietly, so as to be able to hear the ancient silence of some of the oldest exposed rocks of our planet.

But the trail was too popular; several other women came along and stopped to talk. I gave up and gave in, and followed them to the dining room. Dinner consisted of huge slabs of steak, baked potatoes, salad and vegetables, corn bread and chocolate cake. Everything had been carried in on the backs of mules; all trash must likewise be carried back out.

Sitting together on long tables in assigned groupings, we got to visit with others who'd made this trip, either by foot or mule. Stories were diverse and heroic, and most of the folks were over fifty, some even sixty and others were well into their seventies: everyone who makes it here really had to make an effort, as the only ways in are by foot, by mule, or, in the warmer months, by raft. We were truly the chosen ones; those who have chosen to be here...taken the risks, endured the discomfort, and just plain been blessed.

Dinner was over early enough: there was still an hour of daylight, so I headed back to the River. Turning east towards the mule bridge, I wandered down onto the boat beach.

The sand was soft and cool and comforting on my bottom; the solitude and silence were delicious. Looking up the Canyon walls along the river corridor was like being in a womb/tomb enclosure....inhaling the scent of the nearby mud, I gave myself over to fully being here.

The sound of the water, the sight of the earth layers rising above me, the scent of the air, the aftertaste of dinner, the pervading sense of changing light all came together in a moment of deep meditation. And mystery. And magic!

Suddenly, great sobs welled up until I was shaking uncontrollably. A sense of being embedded within everything was so strong that I no longer knew where I ended and the sand and the River and the Canyon began. A supreme knowing of a wholeness akin to holiness swept through me with a relief that was stronger than the grief of all previous losses, disappointments, failures, frustrations. As I let go to go into that place, a strange new power pervaded my being.

In the deep silence, I could hear the River pulsing through my own veins. I could feel the memory of the earth crouched deep within my own DNA. My own breaths interconnected me with the exhalations of the vegetation beside me.

And the light, the glorious, waning light from the sun became the same light from the very beginning of Time itself, reaching me just then. I was one with it all. All was a gift, wrapped up in a moment of grace.

This 'grace-point' is the place where the mystics of all traditions live. As Huston Smith revealed in a lecture I attended in Berkeley: if you put the major religious traditions in side-by side-columns, then draw a line across them all about a third of the way down, this is the line where all the mystics sit, and from where they reflect upon the same Unitive experience.

How right they all were: Jung, Tillich, Emerson, the Hindu Sages. There IS a Ground of Being, a central fire, an Oversoul, a Brahman. Their intuitive insights were as solid as Canyon walls!

Yet the reality of this Canyon was more actual than abstract, something as solid as a pebble I could hold in my hand, while simultaneously being held within the womb of the Universe.

As with all aha moments, this knowing started to fade as my mind began to wander, and my wonder turned into wondering.

Somewhere behind me, the Bright Angel Creek was tumbling down the Bright Angel Fault from the North Rim into the Colorado River; we have followed the Bright Angel Trail from the South Rim to reach this convergence that John Wesley Power named from a favorite Methodist hymn in his childhood.

Shall we gather at the river,
Where bright angel's feet have trod,
With its crystal tide forever,
Flowing by the throne of God.

Which was more ironic: that the hymn's author was a contemporary of the Transcendentalist Emerson, and that he composed it out of a vision that came to him while he was sitting on a couch inside his house? Or this: that it was sung at the funeral of Justice William O. Douglas, a Supreme Court defender of the natural world!?

Still scarcely able to believe I was finally here, I sat drinking in the stillness and listening to this river of life until it was dusk, and time to head back to my cabin while I could still find the trail.

Rather than mythical angels, mysterious bats kept me company, those clever little mammals the Universe evolved in order to experience flight.

With dwindling water reserves, there was no show-ering, so I washed up with a washcloth and climbed into the bottom bunk by 8 pm. I didn't want to sleep, just lie awake for as long as I could.

After all, I had only 18 hours to be here, 10 of which would be dark. On a table beside the cot sat the hotel copy of the Gideon Bible, with its evangelical promotion of a cosmology that suddenly felt more than 2000 years out-of-date!

Reading my worn copy of Brian Swimme's *The Earth Is A Green Dragon* that I 'd stashed in my saddlebag, I dozed off, then reawakened well before midnight.

Perfect! Bundling up, I stepped outside into the deep darkness. A handful of stars were visible in the slice of sky so high above the Canyon walls that it felt like I was looking through a reverse telescope: they appeared to be so far away.

Staring upward, I paid silent tribute to Giordano Bruno, a Dominican monk who came to believe that our sun was a star. For trying to align his Christian theology with the Copernican view of a sun-centered universe, and after a seven-year trial by the Inquisition, he was burned at the stake in 1600 for his heretical belief that the Universe and God are ultimately identical. "Out of this world we cannot fall," he had exclaimed.

Out under the far-away stars as midnight turned yesterday to today, I celebrated my birthday and Bruno's death day simultaneously.

I sensed the power of the Universe locked in the embrace of the igneous rocks that were formed from the molten material within the Earth's interior that came to the surface, intruded into the metamorphic rock, then bubbled up and laid down in layers that have been 'morphed' by heat and pressure into something else.

I made a wish that I too might be transformed into something else by the experience of being Here, so very briefly, in this Now.

Back in the cabin but too excited to sleep, in spite of being anxious about being alert enough to ride the mule back up to the Rim in the morning, I stayed awake listening to the creek, to the rain, to an airliner high above, awaiting the dawn when our star the sun is reborn as the vitality of the earth. The same solar energy that gathered itself up to swim and walk and fly over so many millennia ago continued today, within this human.

Joining the hikers in the first breakfast seating, I marveled at how wondrous was the meal of eggs and bacon and fruit and bread that would fuel our nine-mile trek up and out of the Canyon. I hoped the mules were having a good breakfast too.

Although it was raining when the hikers left in the semi-darkness, by the time we'd mounted up there were patches of blue above us. The rain had ended, leaving the sweet smells of the deciduous cottonwoods budding out, and the striking sight of the Zoroaster Granite glowing pink.

Being the last one Sherry helped onto a mule worked for me as a birthday present. Another gift was the relief of finding that going up was easier on the legs than was the coming down.

Instructed to lean forward, we worked with gravity so as not to hurt the mules' backs.

Short Cut hugged the inner part of the trail, thus brushing me up against the rock walls, so that I got to reach out to receive their blessing.....for my birthday, I flatter myself, recalling Muir's "Climb a mountain and get its glad tidings."

Is it only humans who can appreciate what we were experiencing here while ascending the pages of the planet? We moved slowly through the missing eras known as the Great Unconformity and on through the age of pre-dinosaurs and then into the wildflowers of more recent times with their production of seeds that concentrated energy for higher metabolic creatures such as us.

The mules plodded upward, clearly bored, then stood side by side facing into the Canyon for frequent periods of rest.

I was grateful for every step Short Cut took through the mud that I didn't have to. At one of these stops, Sherry asked what animal can never become extinct via natural selection, and then revealed how the mule is not a natural animal but is created by breeding a jackass with a horse, going on to describe how the mules are bred for the Canyon trips then brought here to be trained by the wranglers...who then got to name them.

One of the names included *Helen Keller*, newly retired. Other names seriously considered but not chosen were *Thelma and Louise* for a pair of females that were inseparable.

Our adventure ended with each of us clutching a scrolled piece of faked parchment that read, in part:

> ...*having faced the precipices, descended and ascended the perpendicular walls at and in the South Rim of the Grand Canyon, endured the vicissitudes of this magnificent journey, and borne the whims and caprices of [her] gentle, faithful, educated, individualistic, long-haired mount-part horse, part jackass, and all mule...*

I staggered on home, numb but happy. Even when the numbness wore off and the pain gripped my muscles for weeks, I realized that rather than having "been to the mountain top," I had been to the bottom of things...

6

GLIMPSING ANOTHER REALITY

"There is a vast entity, a unified reality outside us and within us in which we live and move, a reality that has an intelligible nature."

–Rev. Lex Crane

WHENEVER ANYONE ASKED WHAt the mule trip to the bottom of the Grand Canyon was like, I described it as being 'not unlike childbirth.' The trip down is a bit like the first birthing experience: it is painful, and resistance makes it worse.

This was complicated by not knowing how long it will last, not having ever been on that path before, and thus having no clue if one will be able to make it through. (I will not mention the feet in the stirrups analogy.)

The trip back up was a lot like giving birth to a second child: the pain is familiar, you know how to work *with* it, and you know it will end. You *can* make it through. There was a difference, of course: I got to keep my two daughters; I didn't get to keep the mule. Just as well! For the trip was not about giving birth, but rather about being born into a another view of reality, one that literally came out of the Cosmic Ground of All Being.

With my sabbatical time winding down, I would try to move from watching sunrises and sunsets and into a sense of participating in these as daily cosmic events, and then on towards living in that dimension as fully as possible.

Yet whenever I went out to greet the sun and the gift of a whole new day at the Canyon, it was hard to find a solitary spot where I could tap back into that sense of cosmic connectedness.

With the influx of tourists for spring break vacations, there was always, at all times, the incessant sound of voices…as if we the people can never shut up…I 'prayed' for compassion towards my species, and especially for the impatient, oblivious, irreverent, obnoxious tourist that I was fifteen years ago…

I found myself walking on animal trails and despairing that the Universe had wasted a year of time and energy calling me into this new knowing that now I didn't know what to do with.

As I rested on a sunny rock between Mojave and Hopi Points, the red-tagged black condors appeared, rose up from the Canyon to frolic over my head, and disappeared back down again.

Were they mocking, or challenging, me?

As I began my final sabbatical season, I kept my daily appointment with the dawn's pink streaks: in the beginning was the sun calling forth all life on the planet. I sat sheltered from the cold wind by a 250 million year old rock and drank coffee out of a double walled aluminum mug amidst fossils, knowing they were so that we could be. A whole new perspective shot through with the first rays of the sun, then became too glaring to see anything of what was unfolding.

As light split the dark edges of night and thus length-ened the days, which is what the season of Lent originally referred to, time moved from the winter solstice towards the spring equinox. The Christian world celebrated this as the forty days Jesus spent in the desert preparing for his ministry. Then Palm Sunday's welcome of Jesus as a prophet of the new who threatened those profiting from the old served as a reminder of the risk in shifting one's perspective. Yet I did it anyway, by focusing on the green patches of new life that peeked through a cover of white snow instead of Maundy Thursday, Green Thursday and The Last Supper.

For the Canyon's glow had grown strangely green from all the moisture of the winter as the mystery of spring's new life burst forth from winter's death. Tiny wildflowers bravely showed their shy purple and yellow faces.

Of course Maundy Thursday was also the Passover story, yet another persistent human narrative of being called out of bondage to the old and being reborn into the new. We did know how to move from one state of being into another!

On Good Friday there was snow in the morning, filling the Canyon and sky, though the moon was visible in its pre-dawn setting. The sunrise was blocked out by clouds, but by noon I had decided on a pilgrimage/hike down a mile of the South Kaibab Trail to OOHAH Point.

With the gifts of evolution in my pockets, cereal and nuts and fruit as concentrated protein that enabled warm-blooded species to evolve (the snakes were still hibernating) and water, the stuff that we're mostly made up of, I ventured forth.

At the Pipe Creek pullout, where I left my car, there was zero visibility: snow and fog filled up the Canyon and spilled over the road...but by the time I laced up my hiking boots and set off along the Rim Trail towards Yaki Point, the sun was breaking through in the classic battle between winter and spring, good and evil, dark and light, all echoing the paradoxes of the planet.

The snow on the ground was a glare by the time I reached the trailhead: the brightening sun (I was without sunglasses) and packed snow made the trail slippery (I hadn't brought crampons either) but the wetness had turned the rocks the most exquisite shades of peach and buff that I had yet seen. I decided to go anyway, glad for the poles to keep me from sliding off the trail, and into oblivion.

Hikers with huge packs kept slipping and falling, but after a quarter of a mile the trail became mud We grew grateful for gravity's grasp of our feet that fastened us to the Earth.

Amid the sun and the mules and the snow and the flowers and the rocks with their fossils, I was physically aware that our planet was in its seasonal cosmic dance with the sun and moon!

The day ended with a full moon rising simultaneously with sun's setting: I was out at Mather Point when the snow relented suddenly and the moon seemed to rise out of a notch in the Canyon. The moon being three days dark paralleled Christ's three days in the tomb,... making this a lunar holiday season that culminated in Easter's sunrise. Yet here solar and lunar, eternal and temporal times vied with a third time: deep time....

Thus on Easter morning I was up and out into the freezing cold that had formed a frost that wouldn't yield to windshield scraper. But I had been looking forward to the famous Easter Sunrise Service at the Grand Canyon, one of several places across the continent where people would gather to greet the Sun on this day. So I gingerly drove in the dark to the Yavapai parking lot and walked the moonlit Rim Trail for a mile to reach Mather Point.

Already somebody was shrieking into Canyon; I heard myself yell "Shut up!"

What if, instead of his own narcissistic echo, the Canyon answered back? What would it say?

As I approached Mather Point, an answer came: recorded Native American flute music echoed off the Canyon walls from loudspeakers, with a few Christian hymns interspersed.

How utterly, absolutely appropriate...especially when the sun began to fill the sky with pink light while "Amazing Grace" was playing. The sun itself directed our attention towards Vishnu Temple, a butte rising in the east. A tall black cross claimed space on the makeshift altar as if humanizing the earth's story of creation, destruction, re-creation, the Sun thus becoming the Son.

We the people, perched on the rocks, were right-sized at long last, alongside the juniper and a mouse. It was not a cold day, and there was no wind. The morning was fresh and clear and lovely: spring seemed to have finally, fully arrived.

The sun rose anew as it did each new day, and people have greeted it long before Christians caught on to that concept. Now tourists from the Land of the Rising Sun broke through the masses and made their way to Rim to take pictures. The wisdom from many of the world's faith traditions seemed to intermingle with a hint of what more might come forth from our collective consciousness.

Yet the stench of diesel fumes wafted down from where the buses were idling for warmth: even in our most sublime moments we thought nothing of ruining the atmosphere that made all life on the planet possible!

The preacher's message was about resurrection rather than resuscitation: how even in a marriage, one goes into counseling not to revive the old but to bring forth something new…for why would you seek the living among the dead. He continued: people came to the Canyon to also be changed, via awe that's the beginning of wisdom.

The service ended with flute notes of "Amazing Grace" echoing through the Canyon as if an amen: In the beginning was the Sun as it is each morning anew for us and for the condors and the bighorn sheep and the people starting down the Bright Angel Trail and the mule deer sitting beside the road…all of us being energized by our star.

It well may be that in the next millennium, religious convictions will be primarily awakened and established by meaningful encounters with the mysteries of the Universe and only secondarily by the study of ancient scripture.

This raised the question: were each of the figures around whom major religions have been formed simply messengers from the Universe for telling its truth through them, the light from the birthplace of the Universe breaking through their awareness …Jesus, Buddha, Shiva, Zoroaster…..?

Hours later, I drove my companion and his life-long best friend out to the Hermit Trailhead: they planned to backpack for five nights within the Canyon; I'd take the car back into the Village. But first I hiked down with them as far as the reptile tracks, passing Indian Paintbrush and many other species of wildflow-ers...'show off!' I shouted at the wildness of the natural world: what was the point of such variety anyway?!

And suddenly there were butterflies!...yet another natural sign of the transformation of the season. A white one seemed to be leading me back up the trail... and into a profound sense of being so close to something sacred that were I to sit still long enough the beauty of it would consume me.

Alone on the Rim later in the day, with the sun set-ting and the moon rising simultaneously at opposite sides of the sky, I stood where I could reach between both: the sun through juniper at my left hand and the moon over Rim on my right...

Then, while I was yet shivering on the Rim instead of sitting in the warmth of my car, all at once a condor rose straight up out of the Canyon in front of me....inches away from my face, nearly touching the top of my head... then soared away. It felt like an interspecies salute.

*   *   *   *

Moving between the spring equinox and the coming summer solstice, I faitihfullly kept my appointment with the rising sun each morning, seeking more glimpses of another reality that showed itself so intermittently here on the Rim.

This sabbatical seemed to have been for experiencing the second meditative stage as described in *How To Meditate* by Lawrence LeShan:

> "We will find ourselves working past the tremendous number of self-created distractions, and beginning to perceive just one thing at a time, considered in itself in our consciousness without comparison or relationships. At that time we will also begin to grow toward a new comprehension of a way of being in the world, a new way of perceiving and relating to reality.

As we comprehend more and more of this, we find that we are coming home to a long-lost part of ourselves, that our zest, vitality, efficiency, capacity to love and relate increase and deepen. We also begin to know that each of us is part of all others, that no one walks alone, and that we are indeed home in, and part of, the universe."

Out in the dawn's first light scraping frost off my car with a Kleenex because I had already removed my snow/ice scraper from the trunk, I was astonished: wasn't this MAY, after all! I was wearing the same layers of clothing that I had in March! None too warm sitting out on my favorite bluff overlooking the Canyon and awaiting the sun's rise, I suddenly I realized it was Mother's Day, and that this Canyon was part of our Earth Mother!

As I snuggled against a fossil encrusted boulder and listened to the birds, past and present came together into one moment of Time.

The same life force that flows through all eras of Time was flowing through me. A mother myself, daughters have come forth through me, granddaughters through them. Holding my biological mother in mind, I remembered my grandmother. And beyond: an awareness that we shared the same DNA of all living things on this planet slowly dawned in my body, mind, spirit.

For but a brief moment, I absolutely knew that the raven overhead was an aspect of my DNA that learned how to fly, and was merely a different manifestation of the mother of all, the matrix, the womb out of which we all came.

To come alive in the sun's growing light was to be in the presence of the sacred in the embrace of deep time, and overwhelmed by a beauty I was unable to fully grasp, only be grasped by.

7

PROMISES TO KEEP

"We are the local embodiment of a Cosmos grown to self-awareness. We have begun to contemplate our origins: star stuff pondering the stars; atoms considering the evolution of atoms; tracing the long journey by which, here at least, consciousness arose. Our loyalties are to the species—all the species—and the planet itself. We speak for earth. Our obligation to survive is owed not just to ourselves but also to that Cosmos, ancient and vast, from which we have sprung."
–Carl Sagan

WHEN THE WHEATON VAN LINES agent phoned to say my load date had been moved from the 7th to the 9th of July, I suddenly had a whole extra day to prepare for my move to my next interim position, in Charleston, South Carolina.

This unexpected 'wiggle room' brought relief from the state I had been in, frantically multitasting in preparation for the move. Now, with two extra days dropped into my lap, how best to spend them?

I had already said good-bye to the congregation and to my Canyon companion. And I had not expected to go back up to the Canyon again…but this was too much like my arrival here to not accept the gift of time and GO.

So I packed up snacks and bottles of water and headed north out of town a final time.

Approaching the Rim amid a line of cars filled with tourists, I realized that I was not the same person who arrived here two years ago.

For one thing, instead of heading for Mather Point, I turned east and drove to the Pipe Creek pullout.

From there I walked west on the paved path towards last year's burn. Along the pavement itself were chalk marks setting out a path into Deep Time. I had come across these carefully spaced lines quite by surprise some weeks earlier.

They began three miles east, at Yavapai Observation Point, but when I inquired about them there, no one had any idea or information about what was going on. By shear accident I discovered that this Trail of Time was being developed by the geologist son of a local congregant who was even able to get me his pamphlet explaining the project.

Replicating Earth's timeline along the Rim was to be a way to provide a sense perspective for tourists unable to get to the bottom of the Canyon.

Now I was following chalk markings forward in time, covering one million years with each step, from the age of the oldest rocks within the Canyon through to the largest explosion of life on the plane, and then onward into the present.

This Trail of Time would eventually be laid out between Yavapai Point and the Village, but the earliest version was on this part of the Rim. It ran beside the once scorched earth that was now awash in wildflowers, bearing witness to earth's natural cycle of regeneration. Fighting off the impulse to pause and ponder this mystery, I kept moving forward in Time until I reached the singular footstep representing our human presence on the planet. Surprisingly, it seemed to be the same spot where I had been overcome by sobbing nearly two years ago! So of course I stopped there again.

Shaded by a scraggly juniper bush, I gazed into the Canyon from human time. As Teilhard de Chardin has suggested, it was sometime during the Pleistocene that something within the human turned back upon itself and took a giant leap forward, thus ushering in the Age of Reflection.

Ultimately, it was within the self-reflective human that the Universe could reflect upon itself!

For if the arc of evolution tended towards increasing complexity and consciousness, then the human mind was indeed the vehicle through which it all became self aware: my singular "I' became the 'eye' of the earth and the 'mind' of the Universe considering and celebrating it all!

Yet that same emerging consciousness had been hijacked by human 'cleverness,' and rather than reflect on the mystery of the whole, people focused on pleasure, power, and profit at the expense of all the other life forms we had co-evolved with. In fact, our current epoch of geological time was being called the Anthropocene. Arguably beginning 200 years ago with the onset of the Industrial Age, we the people have been changing the conditions for our very survival by poisoning the soil, acidifying the water, polluting the air, and releasing CO_2 back into the atmosphere. And in the process, we are driving ourselves and our fellow species into extinction.

Would the Earth soon shuck off us off as another failed experiment? As I peered over the Rim into one billion years of its story, every bone in my body rejected the finality of that scenario.

In the burned-out area just beyond me, death meant the end of life that had been there. But extinction meant the end of birth.

Surely humans didn't have to become a dead-end species! Yet what was clear in the time-developmental sequence I was gazing at was this: each was a once-only event, never to be replicated. Thus there was absolutely no guarantee that humans would ever again come into being. The preconditions would simply never be repeated.

What a tragedy! Such a waste!! All that accumulated knowledge short-circuited from transforming into wisdom. How long, if ever, would another species emerge to wonder at the Canyon's beauty and wonder about its meaning?

While many local folks fantasized about silently dropping off the Canon's edge and into oblivion for their final moment of life, I balked. As my hometown poet Robert Frost once framed it:

"But I have promises to keep. And miles to go before I sleep!" Trusting that I still had 'miles to go' figuratively as well as literally, I vowed to work tirelessly to preserve the integrity of this place and the precious planet that it had come to represent.

But now it was time to leave. I walked back to my car, sobbing.

ABOUT THE AUTHOR

Gail Collins-Ranadive, M.A., M.F.A. MDiv.

By the time the author spent a sabbatical year on the South Rim of the Grand Canyon, she had been a psychiatric nurse, a military wife, a private pilot, a religious educator, a writing teacher, a workshop facilitator, an adjunct professor, and an interim minister. She had also authored two non-fiction books: If You'd Been Born in India (for children), and Finding the Voice Inside.

Four years after her sabbatical, she returned to the Canyon during a personal and professional crisis, seeking guidance. Hiking down to a favorite outcropping of rock, she sat in the deep silence until, as clearly as the voice of a friend over coffee, she heard:

"You are a writer. You need to be writing."

She promptly retired from ministry to focus on the manuscripts that had been shapeshifting on her desk for decades. Since then, she has published *Hopi Birth Morning* (with a Hopi elder), *Light Year, Chewing Sand, Nature's Calling, A Fistful of Stars,* and *Dinosaur Dreaming.*

She also writes the biannual environmental column for *The Wayfarer*, and sponsors the Prism Prize for Climate Literature, both divisions of Homebound Publications.

Mother of two and grandmother of five, she and her partner spend winters at her home in Las Vega and summers at his home in Denver. She is currently working on a memoir and a novel.

ACKNOWLEDGMENTS

I am deeply grateful to Jackie Maugh Robinson for reading this manuscript while in process, and to Sandy Ingham for proofing the earliest version. Plus, there are no words to express how much I appreciate Homebound Publications founder Leslie M. Browning's belief in and support of my work, not only for this one.

LITTLE
BOUND BOOKS

OTHER OFFERINGS TO CONSIDER

Naming the Unnameable by Dr. Rev. Matthew Fox

Companions on the Way by Gunilla Norris

Listen by Francesca G. Varela

To Lose the Madness by L.M. Browning

A Comet's Tail by Amy Nawrocki

A Fistful of Stars by Gail Collins-Ranadive

A Letter to My Daughters by Theodore Richards

Terranexus by David K. Leff

What Comes Next by Heidi Barr

Great Pan is Dead by Eric D. Lehman

How Dams Fall by Will Falk

Falling Up by Scott Edward Anderson

WWW.LITTLEBOUNDBOOKS.COM

LOOK FOR OUR TITLES WHEREVER BOOKS ARE SOLD

HOMEBOUND
PUBLICATIONS

We are an award-winning independent publisher founded in 2011 striving to ensure that the mainstream is not the only stream. More than a company, we are a community of writers and readers exploring the larger questions we face as a global village. It is our intention to preserve contemplative storytelling. We publish full-length introspective works of creative non-fiction, literary fiction, and poetry. *Fly with us into our 10th year.*

WWW.HOMEBOUNDPUBLICATIONS.COM